Pa

M000160245

The Wise Preacher

The Story of Paul
Accurately retold from the Bible
(from the book of Acts and Paul's Epistles),
by Carine Mackenzie

Illustrations by
Duncan McLaren
Cover design by Daniel van Straaten

© copyright 2008 Carine Mackenzie
ISBN 978-1-84550-382-6
Reprinted 2014
Published in Great Britain by
Christian Focus Publications
Geanies House, Fearn, Tain, Ross-shire, IV20 1TW, Scotland.
www.christianfocus.com

Printed in China

Saul was born in Tarsus in a Jewish family. He was well educated. He studied in Jerusalem under the scholar Gamaliel. He also learnt the trade of tent-making.

Saul hated those who followed the Lord Jesus Christ. He even threw Christians into jail.

He made a journey to Damascus to imprison some more Christians. On the way an amazing thing happened. A bright light shone from heaven. Saul was terrified.

A voice spoke to him. "Saul, Saul why are you persecuting me?"

"Who are you, Lord?" replied Saul.

"I am Jesus."

Saul was so afraid. "Lord, what do you want me to do?"

"Get up," the Lord said, "and go into the city of Damascus."

Saul was blind and had to be led into the city. For three days he ate and drank nothing, spending his time praying.
God spoke to a follower of Jesus called Ananias telling him where to find Saul.

Ananias was nervous. He knew what Saul had done in the past. God reassured him. "Brother Saul," Ananias said, "the Lord Jesus who appeared to you on the road has sent me so that you may receive your sight and be filled with the Holy Spirit." Immediately Saul could see. He was then baptised, as a sign of his changed life.

He started preaching that Jesus is the Son of God. The followers of Jesus were amazed and delighted, but the Jews plotted to kill him. Saul escaped at night. He was let down the city wall in a large basket.

Saul's life changed completely. Even his name was changed to Paul. Everywhere he went he preached boldly about Jesus. Many people came to trust in Jesus Christ. But there was also great opposition.

Paul and Barnabas were chosen by the church leaders to travel as missionaries and preach the gospel in other countries.

They sailed to the island of Cyprus. The governor, Sergius Paulus, listened to them preach. An evil man called Elymas tried to stop the governor from believing. Paul spoke severely to him. Elymas was struck blind. Sergius Paulus believed the gospel that Paul had preached.

This gospel is still preached today – Jesus Christ died for the ungodly: he died to save us from our sins. This is the good news or Gospel that gives us hope if we trust in him.

Paul and Barnabas moved on through Asia, stopping to preach and set up churches in many different towns.

At Lystra they met a man who had been crippled from birth. Paul saw that he had faith to be healed. "Stand up on your feet," he ordered. Immediately he jumped up and walked.

When the people saw what Paul had done they started worshipping Paul and Barnabas as gods. Paul and Barnabas were so distressed. "We are just men like you," they protested. "You should only worship the living God, the Creator."

When other men arrived the mood of the
people changed. They started to throw
stones at Paul, dragged him out of the city
and left him for dead. Paul recovered and
left Lystra the next day to continue his
work.

After another big journey, Paul, Silas and others reached the seaport of Troas. One night Paul had a vision. A man stood before him and pleaded "Come over to Macedonia and help us."

Paul realised that God was calling them to travel over to Europe.

They arrived at the city of Philippi. On the Sabbath day they went out to the riverside to speak to the women who gathered there to pray.

Lydia listened to Paul's preaching and the Lord opened her heart to accept the truths of the gospel. She trusted in Jesus as her Saviour. She was baptised and her family too. She persuaded Paul and his friends to stay at her house.

If we trust in the Lord Jesus and what he has done, he will be our Saviour also.

A demon-possessed slave girl told fortunes to provide money for her masters. She walked after Paul day after day, shouting. Paul commanded the evil spirit to come out of her. Her masters were very angry and had Paul and Silas thrown into prison.

Paul and Silas still sang praises to God even although they were in chains. Suddenly there was a great earthquake. The doors opened. The chains were loosed. The jailer was so alarmed he was about to kill himself.

"Don't do yourself any harm" cried Paul. "We are all here."
Trembling the jailer asked, "What must I do to be saved?"
"Believe on the Lord Jesus Christ and you will be saved," they told him.
The jailer and his family came to follow Jesus.

Paul spent some time in the big city of Athens. He was upset to see how the people there worshipped idols. He had long discussions in the synagogues and in the market place every day.

Paul told them about Jesus and the resurrection, explaining that Jesus had died and risen again. "God has commanded all men everywhere to repent," he said.

Some of the listeners mocked Paul. Some said, "We will hear about this later." But a few people did believe, including Dionysius and a lady called Damaris.

Trouble met Paul in Ephesus too. He had been preaching for over two years there. Many heard about the Lord Jesus and confessed that they now trusted in him. Some gave up the evil practices of magic, burning their books in public.

Demetrius, a silversmith, earned a lot of money by making silver shrines for the heathen goddess, Diana. With so many people turning to serve God, Demetrius was out of pocket. He roused up a riot in Ephesus against Paul and his companions.

The town clerk managed to calm down the crowd and Paul and his friends were able to leave.

Paul and his companions stopped off for a week in the town of Troas. On the first day of the week the followers of Jesus gathered together. Paul preached to them. He had to leave the next day so he carried on preaching for a long time in the upstairs room, lit by many lights.

A young man called Eutychus sat on the window sill but as Paul preached on and on, Eutychus grew sleepy.

At midnight he slipped over from his perch on the window sill and fell from the third storey to the ground below.

When the people rushed to Eutychus, he was picked up dead.

When Paul reached him, he threw his arms around him. "Don't be alarmed," he said to the crowd. "He's alive."

They all went back upstairs and ate some food together.

Paul carried on talking until daylight, when he had to continue on his journey. Everyone was so pleased that Eutychus was safe and well.

Paul and his friends made their way back to Jerusalem. They were warmly received by the members of the church. Paul told them all about what God had done to bring people in many places to trust in the Lord.

But not everyone was glad to see Paul. Some evil men planned to kill him. A riot broke out as they dragged Paul from the temple, beating him.

The commander of the Roman army heard about the trouble, and at once took soldiers to quell the riot. The commander arrested Paul and had him taken to the barracks.

He was given an opportunity to speak to the crowd, telling them about his life and conversion. The crowd were so angry. All through this Paul remained calm, trusting in God.

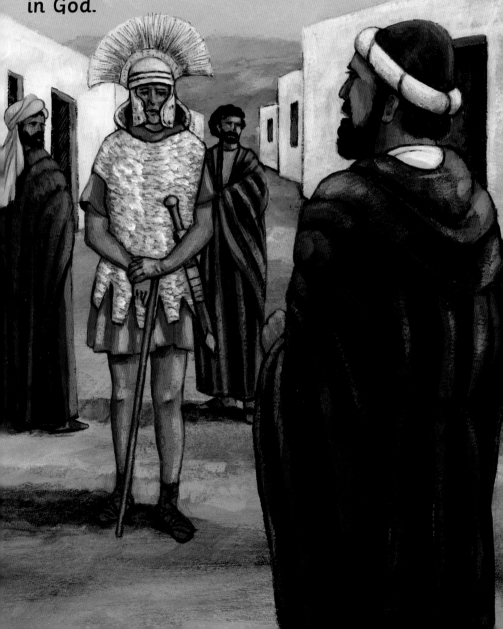

The army commander could not understand why the people were so much against Paul. He was sent first to the group of Jewish leaders called the Sanhedrin. Paul spoke wisely to them but a violent disagreement blew up among the leaders.

Paul was then transferred in the middle of the night to Caesarea to be tried by the governor Felix. He listened to Paul's story, even heard him preach about righteousness and God's judgement to come. However, Felix was not brave enough to let Paul go.

Paul lived in Caesarea for two years, still under arrest but free to preach about the Lord Jesus.

When a new governor, Festus summoned
Paul before him, Paul appealed to Caesar
the Roman Emperor, hoping for justice.
"You will have to go to Rome," declared
Festus.

Paul and other prisoners were put on a ship under the charge of Julius a Roman centurion. The first port of call was Sidon where Paul was allowed to meet up with some friends, then on past Cyprus, heading towards Italy. The weather was very stormy. The journey was difficult and dangerous. But Paul was confident in God who had promised he would reach Rome safely.

The ship was wrecked off Malta but everyone on board made it to the shore. Some swam while others floated on broken planks from the ship. God's promise was true. An angel of the Lord had spoken to Paul, telling him that none of his ship-mates would be lost.

God was looking after Paul even in these difficulties and dangers. God is still the same. Nothing happens without his knowledge and control.

Paul stayed for about three months in Malta till the winter was past. Then they sailed on to Rome, where he was kept under arrest.

Many people came to visit him and listened to his teaching about the kingdom of God. He taught them about Jesus from the books of the Old Testament. Some people believed what he said about Jesus but others would not believe.

Paul stayed for two years in his own rented house, meeting many people and preaching and teaching boldly.

Paul wrote many letters while he was in Rome. We can read them in the Bible. He wrote to the church groups in Colosse, Philippi, Ephesus and Galatia.

He wrote personal letters to Philemon and to Timothy. These letters contain valuable teaching, loving encouragement, wise correction and grateful thanks and appreciation.

Paul was not afraid of dying. "For me to live is Christ but to die is gain," he said.

He was confident in God to the end. "I have fought the good fight," he could say. "I have finished the race. I have kept the faith. Now there is waiting for me in heaven a crown of righteousness."

Paul was a brave missionary, travelling widely, facing many dangers.
He was often in prison, beaten severely, lashed, stoned, shipwrecked. He went without sleep, was hungry and thirsty, cold and uncomfortable.

But he thought it all worthwhile for the privilege of preaching the gospel of God. Everywhere he went he told the wonderful news that Christ had died for the ungodly.

Everyone is ungodly. We must trust in the same Saviour that Paul trusted in. "By grace you are saved," Paul tells us, "through faith. Not by any good thing we might do."

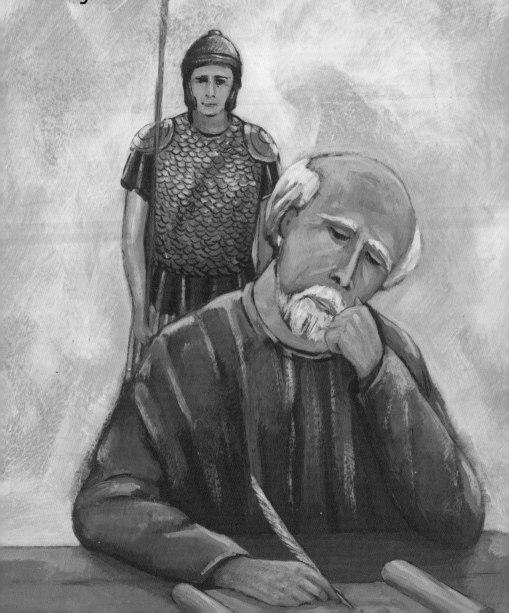